THE DEMISE OF TONTO
OR
HOLLYWOOD MEETS THE SIOUX

*"TO TRANSFORM 100 MOVIE EXTRAS INTO WARRIORS
WEARING BUCKSKIN, WAR PAINT, & FEATHERS,
AND THEN TO SEE THEM ON HORSEBACK SILHOUETTED
AGAINST THE HORIZON OF AN EPIC LANDSCAPE –
THAT IS THE MAGIC THAT KEEPS ME IN THE ART OF
MOTION PICTURE COSTUME DESIGN"*

CATHY A. SMITH

THE DEMISE OF TONTO
OR
HOLLYWOOD MEETS THE SIOUX

Copyright © 2017 by Cathy A. Smith

ISBN 978-1-944293-18-5

COSTUME DESIGN

IS ABOUT STORYTELLING - ABOUT BRINGING A VISION TO LIFE.

THIS IS MY STORY

Cathy Smith on location - *Dances with Wolves*

Cathy Smith is an artist and historian of the American West, with expertise in beadwork and porcupine quillwork. She is best known for the authentic costumes she made for films including *Dances with Wolves*, *Geronimo*, *Comanche Moon*, and *Son of the Morning Star*, for which she won the Emmy Award for Excellence in Costume Design.

But more than that, Cathy is a bridge between cultures - the Native American and Hollywood.

Her costumes are not really "costumes" - they're the real thing, transporting the power and beauty of Native regalia to the world.

Based on impeccable historical research, they bring a character to life with authenticity and credibility.

Smith has spent her lifetime participating in the ceremonies and cultural life-ways of her family on the Cheyenne River Sioux Reservation and refining her skills in the sacred art of porcupine quillwork, so that what she brings to film is true, rich in detail, and steeped in history.

As well as costuming films, she lectures on the art & culture of the West at museums and events around the world and has exhibited at museums from the Smithsonian, the Eiteljorg, and the Booth, to the Wolakota Conference in Florence, Italy.

Smith restores Plains Indian artifacts for museums and collectors, has consulted on a majority of the western genre films of the past 25 years, and is a recent inductee into the National Cowgirl Museum & Hall of Fame - recognized for her courage and pioneer spirit.

She has a studio in the Black Hills of South Dakota and in Nambe, New Mexico where she and her daughter, fine jeweler - Jennifer Jesse Smith, have revitalized the historic Nambe Trading Post. Located on the High-Road to Taos, the trading post displays many of Smith's costumes.

Paul Rainbird
Former Director of the Institute of American Indian Arts Museum
Santa Fe, New Mexico

Cathy Smith and the Dalton Gang in *Gunfighters of the West*

My specialty is Western and Native American costume. This interest did not originate in Hollywood, but on a ranch near the Cheyenne River Sioux Reservation where I was raised - surrounded by Cowboys and Indians, the Real Thing! I was born in Deadwood, Calamity Jane and Wild Bill were my heroes. My paternal grandfather raised cavalry remount horses for old Fort Meade and my 'Hunka Ina" or great grandmother was an Assiniboin Sioux Holy Woman.

I grew up on the stories of the Old-timers - the tales of Crazy Horse and Old Man Afraid of His Horse, and when they told of the medicine men who could turn a bullet or make the sun leave the sky, it was magical.

Making movies is another kind of magic, or it can be when the right elements come together. For me the early Westerns were an embarrassment: John Wayne fought white men dressed as Indians, Tonto, or even a Man Called Horse looked ridiculous in faux leather. This was the Myth of the West in Technicolor, a popular image of a frontier that never was, nor were the costumes historically accurate.

Dances with Wolves, shot in 1989, was among the first films to portray Indians in all their humanity and complexity. And I believe it to be the first time Native costumes and sets were historically accurate. We were given ten weeks to create all of the costumes from scratch, including doubles and triples for stars and stunts. A crew of six, we worked fifteen hour days, seven days a week to hand-sew, bead and quill the buckskin costumes.

Then of course, the costumes must be 'aged' or given a patina so that they would look worn and lived in.

Research for *Dances with Wolves* involved studying the journals and illustrations left by early explorers and native drawn pictographs. Since our time period was pre-camera there were no historical reference photos available.

Brain tanned buckskin was the material of choice in the 1850's. To create it, hides are softened with the brains of the animal, resulting in a soft, pure white hide, which was often smoked to give it color and water resiliency. Our first job was to find more than 600 deer hides with the look of brain tanned hide.

Graham Green and Rodney Grant in *Dancing with Wolves*

PORCUPINE QUILLED WARSHIRT

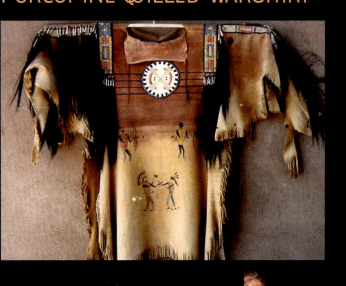

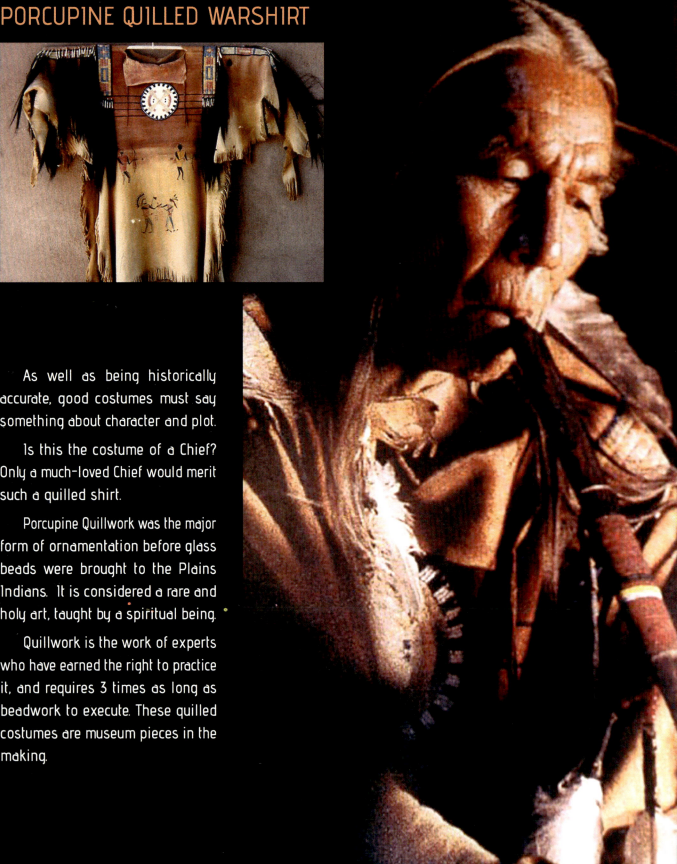

As well as being historically accurate, good costumes must say something about character and plot.

Is this the costume of a Chief? Only a much-loved Chief would merit such a quilled shirt.

Porcupine Quillwork was the major form of ornamentation before glass beads were brought to the Plains Indians. It is considered a rare and holy art, taught by a spiritual being.

Quillwork is the work of experts who have earned the right to practice it, and requires 3 times as long as beadwork to execute. These quilled costumes are museum pieces in the making.

QUILLWORK

Plucking quills from a porcupine hide in preparation for the quilled shirt rosette below.

The rosette is edged with "pony beads," the first glass beads brought in trade by European trappers. The beads were hand-blown glass made in Murano, Italy.

All of the beads I use in my pieces are original stock Venetian glass from the 19th century.

Smith repairing a stunt costume on the set of
Dances with Wolves.

When the shooting starts the real fun begins.
The Costumer is always on the set ready to repair
or make adjustments to costumes in action.

Since a film is never shot in sequence, a continuity
book is kept with photos and descriptions of each
scene. We might shoot Scene 25 this morning and
Scene 90 this afternoon, so someone has to keep
track of how many feathers were in Kicking Bird's
hair and at what angle, how dirty the shirt was,
etc., so that when we shoot the following scenes
weeks later we get the continuity right.

A day in the life of filming *Dances with Wolves* began at 3:30 AM on location in a 65,000 acre buffalo pasture, fifty miles from Ft. Pierre, South Dakota.

How fast can we dress 150 men, women, and children in period garments? Dressing in tents in the pre-dawn twilight, we tie up leggings, hide bra straps, remove watches and modern jewelry and get everyone through wardrobe and into hair & makeup

And just because someone is a registered member of the Lakota nation does not mean they know how to put on a breechcloth!

Meanwhile the stars are being dressed in their trailers and going over their lines, I'm finishing the last bit of beadwork on Stand with a Fit's dress and our director, Kevin Costner is setting up the first shot.

Mary McDonnell & Kevin Costner in Summer Camp on DWW.

Both actresses wear pony-beaded brain tanned buckskin dresses, ornamented with brass Hudson Bay trade buttons and elk teeth respectively.

Kevin Costner, Rodney Grant, and Graham Green.

STUNTS

Adam Beach, Wes Studi, and stuntman Dutch Lunak in *COMANCHE MOON*

Blue Duck lances Buffalo Hump: How it's done!

The lance fits into the socket in his back.

STUNTS require special costumes – they must be made strong enough to withstand violent action and often fire-proofed. If a scene calls for blood, an arrow or bullet hit – 5 or 6 copies of each costume must be made. This is as hard on the costume maker as it is on the budget.

We never get it in one take!

Each principal actor has a stunt double who must have identical costumes and sometimes we have to quickly improvise, as seen in the photo below!

Above: Fire scene in *Comanche Moon*
Below: Robert Pasterelli as Timmons in *DWW*

Stuntman Tom Berto doubles as a woman.

THE PAWNEE

Wes Studi and the Boys

Above: Kate Bighead in *Son of the Morning Star*
Below: Mary McDonnell in *DWW*

Delphine High Hawk & Darlene Young Bear –
My Auntie and my Mom had parts in *Dances with Wolves*

SON of the MORNING STAR won an EMMY for Costumes in 1991.

The story of Custer and Crazy Horse and the Indian Wars, this is the only time
date, that Native American costumes have won an Academy Award.

Custer's 7th Cavalry rides toward the Little Big Horn while Crazy Horse
(Rodney Grant) paints his face for battle.

Cheyenne Dog Soldier

Lakota war bonnet warrior

Cathy Smith just finished Red Cloud's
War bonnet

Red Cloud's War shirt & Leggings

My biggest challenge on *Son of the Morning Star* was the portrayal of Crazy Horse, a hero of mythic proportions among the Lakota.

He never allowed his photograph to be taken, so we have no image to refer to. I replicated a shirt attributed to Crazy horse that is in storage in the Smithsonian.

Rodney Grant as Crazy Horse

Doris Leader Charge, Lakota language teacher

Rodney Grant as Crazy Horse

Custer burns the Cheyenne village on the Washita River

In more than 35 films, some better than others, I have created the most authentic costumes possible, in the unbelievably short time allowed, while at the same time, supporting the image of each character and pleasing the director. Sometime directors don't care about authenticity - it's more about their vision; Then we have a discussion.

I am often a consultant for other designers and make costumes for their films. It is impossible to do the research required to make authentic native costumes in the few weeks of pre-production - this is where my lifetime of research pays off.

I believe it is extremely important for Hollywood to treat another culture with respect, depicting them truthfully - film lasts forever.

Geronimo, An American Legend, directed by Walter Hill was extremely authentic, with the exception of the location in Monument Valley. Geronimo's war cap below is an exact replica of the original in storage at the Gene Autrey Museum. I had the great honor to examine the original.

Wes Studi as Geronimo

Shooting a Western is always a challenge. When choreographing wild animals, horses, buffalo, wolves, and "wild Indians" out in the prairie weather, anything can happen and it's seldom in your control.

Above: Comanche Raiders pose with Smith during filming of *Lightning Jack*.
Below: The buffalo are first seen in *Dances with Wolves*.

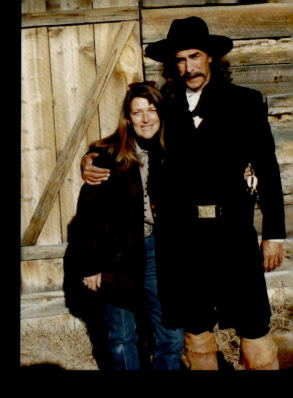

Angelica Huston as Calamity Jane,
Peter Coyote as Buffalo Bill,
Reba McEntire as Annie Oakley

Top Right: Smith & Sam Elliot
as Wild Bill Hickok.

Lower Right: Smith & Peter Coyote

Top: Russell Means as Sitting Bull.
Wes Studi as Comanche chief
Buffalo Hump

Bottom: Comanche raid Austin

Above: *Gunfighters of the West*

Right: *Comanche Moon*

Prince Maximilian zu Wied, Atlantis Films, Berlin, traced the Prince's 1832 journey of discovery into the wilds of the Upper Missouri. Meeting the Mandan chief Mato Tope, whose portrait Karl Bodmer painted, is one of the distinctive scenes. The porcupine quilled regalia required 6 months to create and is now on display in a museum in Santa Fe, NM.

Dreidoppel visits Mato Tope's earthlodge

Prince Maximilian w/pistol

Trade scene and fight at Fort McKenzie

Yes, 1 did meet Kevin Costner, 1 worked with him for 5 months

The Glory of the Costumer!

Cathy & Jenny Smith on *Gunfighters of the West*

Cathy Smith on *set of Crazy Horse*

Cathy Smith with the buffalo hunters on *Dances with Wolves*

"Cathy, here we go again!" said Sam Shepard on the set of *"Don't Come Knockin'."*

Costuming a Western is a demanding experience that totally absorbs the designer's life for many months. It requires diligent research, artistic inspiration, creative skill, physical endurance, and a love of the subject. For me, it is a time machine wherein I can go back and live for a time in the past. It is re-creating history. I've fought the Battle of the Little Big Horn at least 6 times, ridden with Geronimo across Monument Valley, chased Lightning Jack through Antelope Canyon and Quanah Parker across the Llano Estacado, and followed Crazy Horse through the Badlands.

The best part is that it is recorded on film forever ~
that is why it is so important to get it right.
Thanks for going to the movies!